KNOW-IT-ALLS

SHARKS!

Written by Irene Trimble
Illustrated by Mike Maydak

Text reviewed by Marcelo R. de Carvalho, Department of Icthyology, American Museum of Natural History.
Art reviewed by Lisa Mielke, Department of Education, New York Aquarium.

Published by
Bendon Publishing International, Inc.
605 Westlake Drive, Ashland, OH 44805
www.bendonpub.com

Long before dinosaurs ruled the land…

SHARKS

hunted the seas. They have survived on earth for 400 million years!

Megalodon

Great White

The now extinct Megalodon shark lived 15 million years ago. It was 40 feet (12 m) long, and its jaws were so large, a man could stand inside them!

Today there are over 375 different kinds, or **species**, of sharks. Marine biologists, the scientists who study ocean life, are still discovering more!

POWERFUL HUNTERS

Sharks have skeletons made of soft, flexible **cartilage** instead of hard bone. (The end of your nose is made of cartilage.)

Instead of smooth scales, sharks have very tough skin covered with tiny barbs called **dermal denticles**.

And they use their strong jaws and many rows of very sharp teeth for biting and tearing!

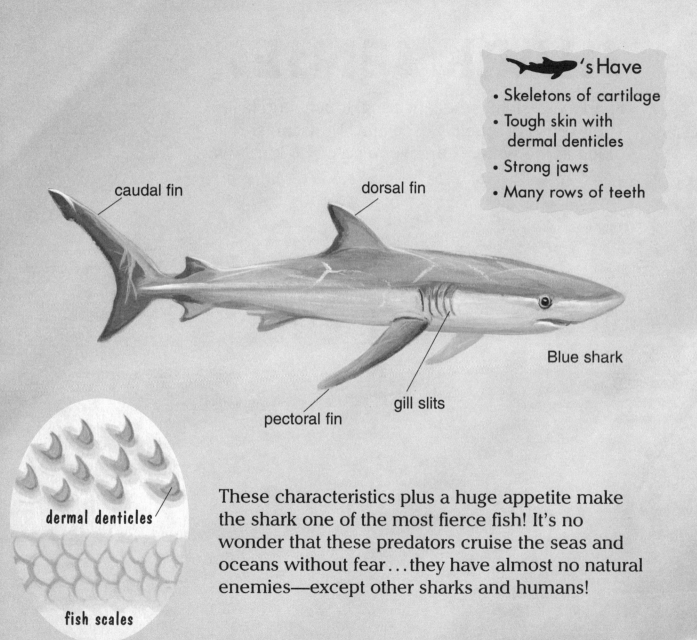

's Have

- Skeletons of cartilage
- Tough skin with dermal denticles
- Strong jaws
- Many rows of teeth

caudal fin

dorsal fin

Blue shark

pectoral fin

gill slits

dermal denticles

fish scales

These characteristics plus a huge appetite make the shark one of the most fierce fish! It's no wonder that these predators cruise the seas and oceans without fear...they have almost no natural enemies—except other sharks and humans!

5

SHARK SENSES

Sharks use sight, smell, hearing, touch, and taste. Their sense of smell is excellent. They can smell blood in the water from over a mile (1.6 km) away!

Tiger shark

White-tip reef shark

Sharks also have sensors, called **ampullae** (am-PUL-ee), in their snouts, and sensitive hairs and channels, called a **lateral line system**, along their sides. These extra senses help them find distant or unseen prey and navigate through the ocean.

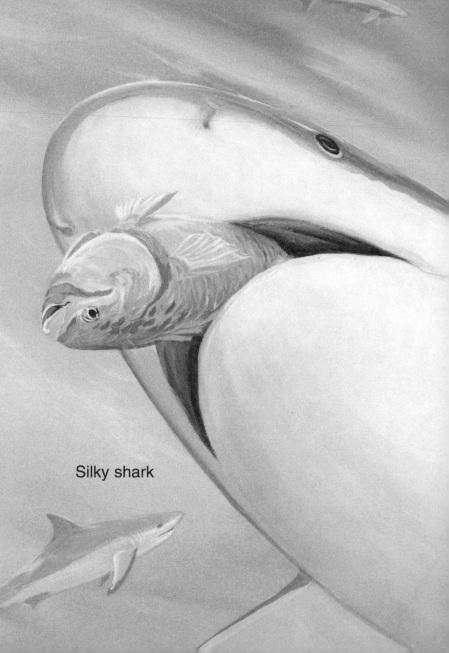

SHARK ATTACK

A shark begins to look for its prey when it is within about 100 feet (31 m). At this point, the shark circles the victim slowly and may even bump into it a few times to see how strong it is. Then the shark quickly picks up speed as it closes in for the attack!

Silky shark

The attack begins as the shark clamps down on its victim with powerful jaws, and shakes its head from side to side to tear out a bite! The smell of blood can cause other sharks to join the attack. They wildly take bites of the wounded fish or animal. This is called a **feeding frenzy**.

BLUE SHARKS

Many shark species travel great distances,
like migrating birds. Blue sharks may be
the farthest ranging, swimming up to 4,000
miles (6,400 km) in about a year!

Like most sharks, baby Blue sharks are born ready
to swim. Young sharks are called **pups**. Female Blue
sharks can give birth to more than 50 pups at a time!

Blue 🦈's
- Length: 12 feet (4 m)
- Diet: fish, squid, and dead whales
- Blue sharks live in warm tropical waters and follow warm ocean currents all over the world.

A few species of shark lay eggs, like other fish.

HAMMERHEAD SHARKS

These sharks swim in gigantic packs of 150 or more! They have wide, flat heads that help them slice through the water.

Hammerhead's

- Length: 3 to 18 feet (1 to 5.5 m)
- Diet: fish and rays
- Hammerheads hunt in the warm waters of South America and Hawaii.

The hammer-shaped heads of these sharks can be up to 3 feet (1 m) wide, with eyes set on each end. (Imagine having eyes that far apart!) As they swim, hammerheads swing their heads from side to side. This motion may help them see more of their surroundings.

TIGER SHARKS

Tiger sharks feed on almost every other fish and mammal in the sea. In fact, they will take a bite out of ANYTHING! License plates, rolls of tar paper, tin cans, and other not-so-very-digestible items have been found in their stomachs!

Tiger sharks have curved teeth with sharp notches, like a steak knife.

Tiger 's

- Length: up to 18 feet (5.5 m)
- Diet: fish, sea turtles, seals, and just about anything else
- Tiger sharks can most often be seen in the Pacific and Indian Oceans.

Tiger sharks have stripes like a tiger. However, their stripes get lighter as they get older!

THRESHER SHARKS

Thresher sharks have the longest tails of any shark. Their tails make up half the length of their bodies!

These sharks move very quickly. They use their long tails to slap schools of small fish. Then they eat the stunned fish that cannot swim away!

Thresher 🦈's

- Length: up to 20 feet (6 m)

- Diet: fish

- Thresher sharks live in warm coastal waters all over the world.

Thresher sharks are not dangerous to people—unless they get slapped by a tail!

WHALE SHARKS

These white-spotted giants are the largest sharks in the world! They grow longer than school buses!

Whale sharks feed at the surface of the water and swim so slowly that boats sometimes bump into them. They are so gentle that divers can catch rides on their backs!

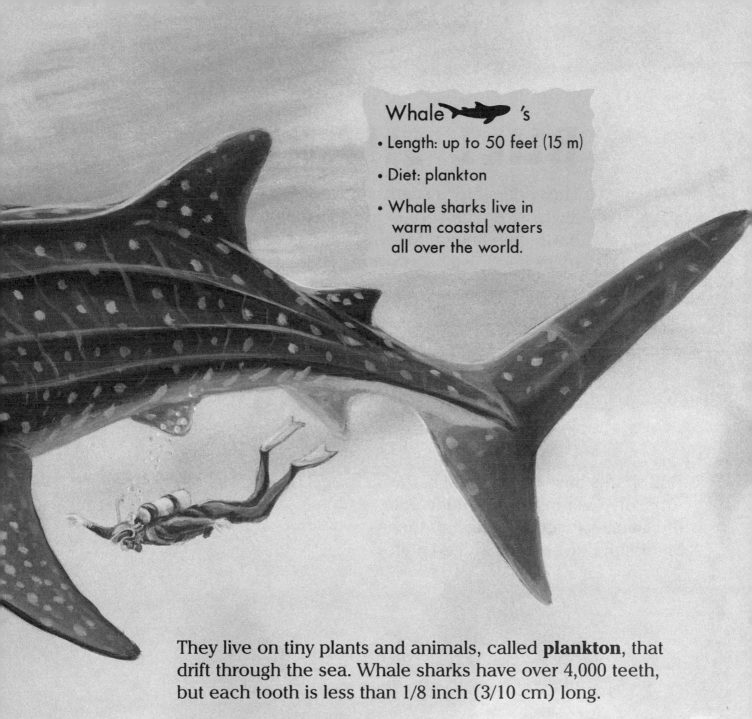

Whale 🦈's

- Length: up to 50 feet (15 m)

- Diet: plankton

- Whale sharks live in warm coastal waters all over the world.

They live on tiny plants and animals, called **plankton**, that drift through the sea. Whale sharks have over 4,000 teeth, but each tooth is less than 1/8 inch (3/10 cm) long.

BULL SHARKS

These dangerous sharks are very aggressive. They live in every ocean and have been known to swim hundreds of miles into freshwater rivers and lakes!

Bull sharks have been found in the Amazon River in South America, the Ganges River in India, and the Mississippi River in the United States!

Bull 🦈's

- Length: up to 10 feet (3 m)

- Diet: fish—and just about anything else

- Bull sharks are found in warm coastal waters worldwide, and in some freshwater rivers.

GREAT WHITE SHARKS

The Great White is one of the largest predators in the sea. Its thick torpedo-shaped body can weigh 2 to 5 tons (2 to 4.5 metric tons)!

These sharks hunt alone, cruising at about 2 miles (3 km) per hour. But Great Whites are very hard for ocean scientists to track. Very little is actually known about these mysterious beasts.

Great White 🦈's

- Length: up to 35 feet (11 m)

- Diet: seals, sea lions, and large fish

- Great White sharks are found all over the world—especially in Australia's Great Barrier Reef.

The Great White's triangular teeth are 2 inches (5 cm) long. Their powerful jaws are filled with many rows of these teeth!

SO MANY SHARKS

Over millions of years, sharks have learned to live in many different underwater environments. Today these silent and mysterious predators come in a variety of shapes and sizes, and they thrive in almost every sea and ocean on earth.

A snowman for Little Bear

Written & Illustrated by
Trace Moroney

SCHOLASTIC INC.

Deep in the woods on a cold winter's morning
Little Bear was snoozing . . . and snoring . . .

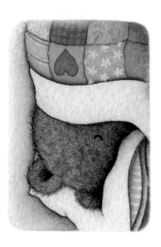

then stretching . . .

and yawning . . .

WHEN . . . something caught her eye.

A big fluffy snowflake floated gently past her window.

The first snow had arrived.

She squealed with excitement.

No one loved snow more than Little Bear.

As fast as **bear**ly possible she put on:

a woolly hat
(with a
pom-pom
on top)

a snuggly
coat

and
finally,
mittens.

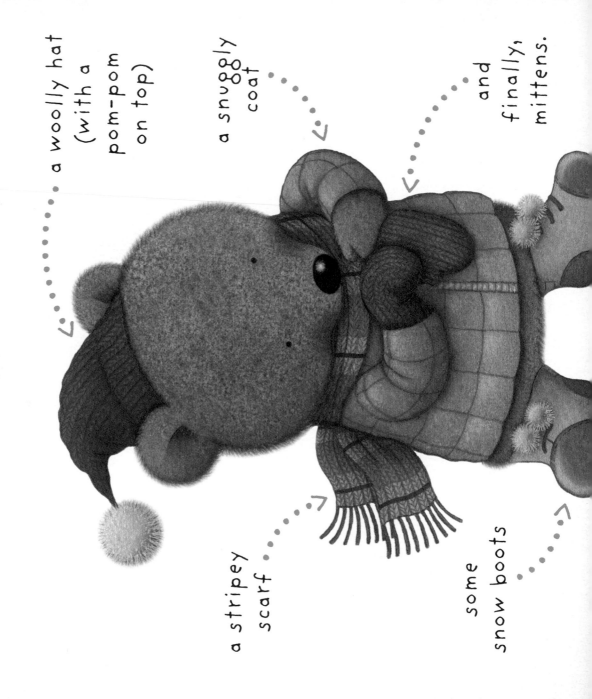

a stripey
scarf

some
snow boots

Then she raced out the door
into the soft, white snow.

Little Bear loved to make dragon's breath in the cold air.

She loved to catch snowflakes on her tongue.

She loved to throw snowballs.

She loved to
make footprints

. . . and follow others.

She loved to go fast on her sled.

She loved to make
snow angels
AND . . .

She especially loved to make a snowman.

After patting
and rolling
and pushing,

and lifting
and huffing
and puffing,

she took a step back to take a look.

"Hmmm . . . I think something is missing."

A family of downy sparrows had gathered to watch
and were excitedly tweeting about
Little Bear's progress.
News traveled fast deep in the woods.

Along came Little Squirrel.

"Look here, Little Bear — I have just the right thing.
A snowman needs some eyes."

"Of course!" Little Bear said as she
clapped her hands with delight.
"But . . . I think something is still missing."

The downy sparrows tweeted as fast as they could.
News traveled fast deep in the woods.

Along came Little Bunny.

"Look here, Little Bear — I have just the right thing. A snowman needs a nose."

"Of course!" said Little Bear, feeling very thankful that Little Bunny would give her one of her precious carrots. "But . . . I think something is still missing."

The downy sparrows tweeted as fast as they could. News traveled fast deep in the woods.

Along came Little Dormouse
(and her seven brothers and sisters).

"Look here, Little Bear — we have just the right thing.
A snowman needs a smile."

"Of course!" said Little Bear, which made her smile.
"But . . . I think something is still missing."

The downy sparrows tweeted as fast as they could.
News traveled fast deep in the woods.

Along came Little Red Fox.

"Look here, Little Bear — I have just the right thing. A snowman needs a scarf."

"Of course!" said Little Bear, admiring the colorful, woolly scarf Little Red Fox's mom had knitted. "But . . . I think something is still missing."

The downy sparrows tweeted as fast as they could. News traveled fast deep in the woods.

Along came Little Owl.

"Look here, Little Bear — I have the last missing thing. A snowman needs a hat."

"Of course!" said Little Bear, agreeing that the snowman was complete . . .

ALMOST . . .

"Wait!" squealed Little Bear,
"there's just one more thing!"
She hurried inside and ... a moment later
returned, carrying something very special.

"Look here," said Little Bear. "I have JUST the right thing!"

And . . . she had.

The downy sparrows tweeted as fast as they could. The **best-ever** snowman had been made in the woods.

Deep in the woods on a cold winter's evening,
Little Bear was stretching . . .

and yawning . . . .

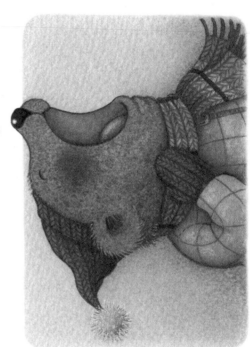

then . . . .

snoozing and ...

zzZZZZZzzz

Cuddly Bear Puppet

Making a sock puppet is an easy and inexpensive way to bring the Little Bear character to life.

While any sock will do, I prefer a super-soft bed sock because it stretches more (it shapes better to your hand) and it is fluffier (it's more like fur), which helps create a character and personality that is warm and cuddly.

Don't worry if your sock has bright colors and patterns that are not particularly bear-like, because you can have lots of fun choosing colors for the ears, arms, mittens, and other parts that you like and that work with the sock.

If you are a crafty person, you may prefer knitting a sock with fluffy wool.

Use the templates provided to create ears, arms, mouth, mittens, and other details or, if you prefer, design your own.

You will need:

A super-soft, fluffy bed sock
Craft felt (in assorted colors) or flexible cardboard
Scissors
Fabric glue
Glue gun (or needle and thread if you prefer to sew)
Pencil or chalk
Eyes (buttons or doll's eyes from a craft store, or small circles cut from black felt)
Pom-pom (for tip of hat)
Remember: Ask for help if you need it and have lots of fun creating your own Little Bear.

Instructions

1. Place the sock over your hand. Your f ngers held together make the top of the mouth (pushed into the toe area of the sock) while your thumb makes the bottom (pushed into the heel area of the sock). Push the area between the toe and the heel back into the crease of your hand, creating the back of the mouth. Practice making the puppet's mouth move by opening and closing your fingers and thumb.
   Optional: If you prefer, insert and glue a cardboard mouth inside the sock. This creates a more rigid mouth area. I prefer not to use it because I am able to create many more funny facial expressions on the puppet's face without it.

2. With your other hand, mark the position of the eyes. Take the sock off, then glue or sew the eyes into position.

3. Using the templates as guides, trace or copy the shapes onto the craft felt. Each ear, each arm, and each mitten is made up of 2 identical felt shapes glued together. So you will need to cut 4 ears, 4 arms, and 4 mittens in your chosen colors.

4. Glue 2 identical pieces together for each part. For example, glue 2 arm shapes together to create a single thicker arm for the puppet. The mittens are glued over the end of the arms.

5. Cut shapes for the mouth, tongue, nose, heart, hat, and scarf from felt in your chosen colors. You only need 1 shaped felt piece for each of these. The tail is simply the top of the toe area of another sock scrunched up, then glued into place.

6. Place the sock back onto your hand and with your other hand mark the position of the ears. Take the sock off, then glue or sew the ears into position. Repeat this process for the mouth, tongue, nose, heart, and scarf.
   Glue or sew the two straight edges of the hat p ece together, then fold up the opening to create a sturdy base. Glue pom-pom on tip, then glue the hat into position.

7. And last but not least . . . give your cuddly bear puppet a great, big bear hug!

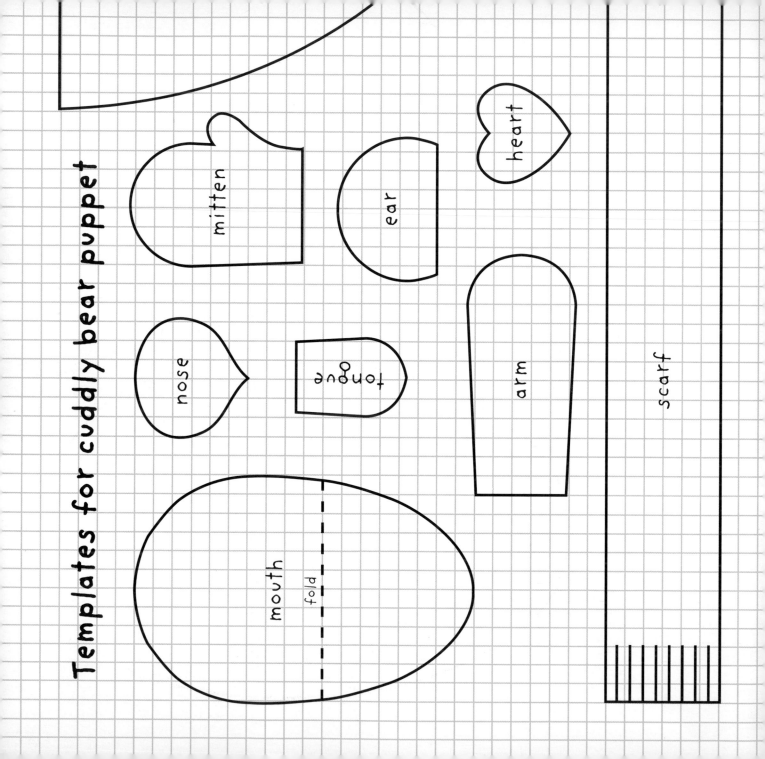

Templates for cuddly bear puppet

mitten

ear

heart

nose

tongue

arm

scarf

mouth

fold

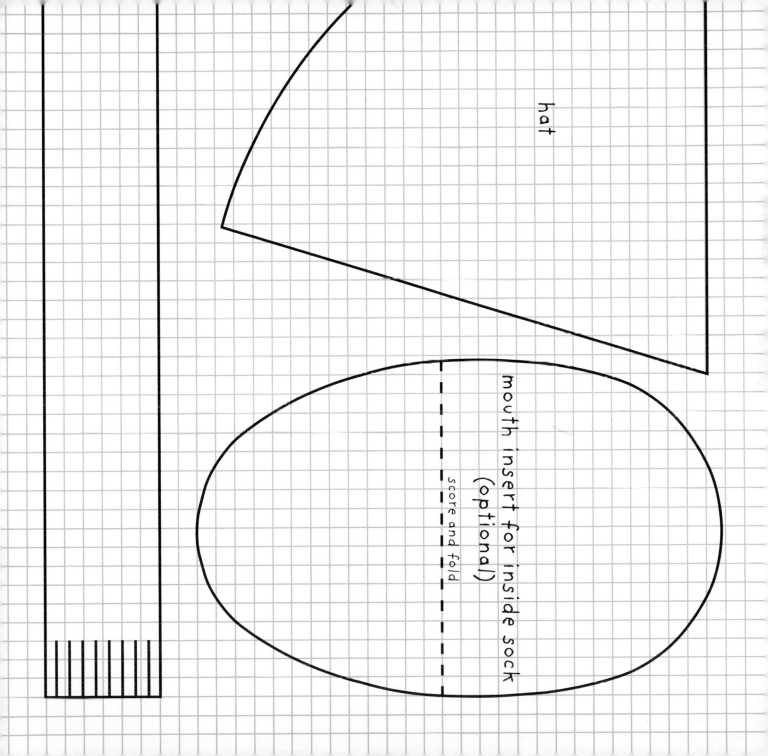

hat

mouth insert for inside sock
(optional)

score and fold